TIME SPACE AND DRUMS PART FIVE

ODD TIME
DRUMMING
Development

TIME SPACE AND DRUMS PART FIVE

ODD TIME DRUMMING Development

TIME WARPS

The Time Space & Drums Series
A Complete Program of Lessons in Professional, Contemporary Rock and Jazz Drumming Styles.

Written and Developed By:
Stephen Hawkins

Graphic Design By: Nathaniel Dasco.
Special Thanks To Linda Drouin and Ikhide Oshoma

ThinkeLife Publications

Time Space and Drums Copyright 2020 By Stephen Hawkins.

All Rights Reserved.

No part of this book may be reproduced in any form or by any electronic or mechanical means including information storage and retrieval means without permission in writing from the author.

The only exception is by a reviewer, who may quote short excerpts in a review.

Stephen Hawkins – Time Space and Drums
Visit my website at www.timespaceanddrums.com

First printing: Jan 2020.

ISBN: 978 1 913929 04 6

Dedicated to the late Paul Daniels and family, Martin Daniels, Trevor Daniels, Paul Mellor's, Keith Richards, Peter Windle, Andrew Marple's, Colin Keys, Peters & Lee, Susan Maughan, Ronnie Dukes, Tom O'Connor, Les Dennis, the late Bob Monkhouse, Bobby Davro, Tommy Bruce, Robert Young, Sandie Gold as well as the hundreds of other people who have played a part in my life experience. Including Sphinx Entertainment, E & B Productions as well as the hundreds of fantastic personalities I have had the pleasure of working alongside over the past 35 years. Apologies for anyone I have missed, not forgetting the current reader who I hope will receive as much from their drumming as I have and more – Stephen Hawkins.

Table of Contents

DRUM ROLL, PLEASE! INTRODUCTION 1

Lesson 1: 3/4, 2/4 & 6/8 Timing 3

Lesson 2: 5/4 Timing 16

Lesson 3: 7/4 Timing 24

Lesson 4: 9/4 Timing 29

Lesson 5: 5/8, & 7/8 Timing 32

Lesson 6: 9/8 Timing 41

    TIME WARPS 44

    RUDIMENTARY 45

Flam Exercises 45

1/8th Note Rhythm and Quarter Note Flams 45

Different Practice Approach 47

    Featured Drummer 48

Conclusion 49

DRUM ROLL, PLEASE!

INTRODUCTION

If you have been following the Time Space and Drums Series, you should by now have an excellent degree of mastery of 4/4 time and playing rock and jazz style rhythms. Your next step is to develop a feel for other time signatures, namely 3/4, 6/8, 2/4, 5/4, 7/4, 9/4, 5/8, 7/8 and 9/8.

In some respects, you are right at the beginning again, in that you are entering new territory once more to begin forming a foundation of skills playing in basic odd time meters.

Throughout this fifth part of the series, you will begin to get a firm grasp of timing in general, and the structure of notation. If you haven't already, I recommend you read the Modern Drumming Concepts book as it discusses an advanced concept to time playing that may help you get a clearer understanding of what time actually is.

Again, these are beginning exercises in foreign time signatures so must be approached in a scientific manner, or mathematically, as should all of the exercises within this series.

Before you can add up, you need to learn the numbers followed by basic arithmetic. Before you can speak a new language, you have to learn the letters, then build simple words and sentences. It is the same with drumming. You need to first learn the letters (notes), the words (basic beats), short phrases (beats and fills), and eventually how to make up your own sentences and so on.

But at the heart of drumming, we need to learn to master time. We must understand that time is something that we create and not something we are obedient to. Again, see the Modern Drumming Concepts book for more information on time, along with the Free Classified Document available by visiting the URL that follows.

So, we now know that before you can play great music, you need to learn the notes and the all-important time. Therefore, when you first learn each exercise given in this book, practice each of them for as long as needed until you have mastered each exercise followed by each complete lesson.

This could be anything from 30 minutes to 30 days. Then...

1. When you can play each lesson and have spent 1 week just practicing that lesson, go through the book until you have completed each lesson over a 6-week period. Spend 1 week on each lesson.
2. Then, go through the book by spending a whole day practicing and striving for greater precision for 6 days, with 1 day per lesson. *(If you are so inclined, you can spend 24 hours on each lesson; of course, that will take more than 1 day practicing 1 hour per day).*
3. Then, go through the whole book in 6 hours.
4. Afterwards, you should go through the book, moving from one exercise to the next, all the time striving for greater precision as you play through the whole book in a single practice session.
5. You can then begin to add technique to the equation to further improve the feel and flow of the exercises.
6. When you are at this point, you should begin your 10,000 hours.

I am sure that by now you understand that you need to spend time developing and mastering these exercises one at a time. So, without further ado, let's get down to the nitty-gritty.

And as usual, we will keep it as simple as possible. This isn't about how many notes you can play in a bar or how fast you can play them. It is about how well you play the notes that you play! It is about time, and space.

Free Audio Demonstrations

You should visit the following URL to download audio demonstrations of every exercise in this book as soon as possible. You will then receive additional tips and guidance through the included essence emails.

https://timespaceanddrums.com/tsd-5ot.html

Second Classified Document

Universal Constants - Philosophy of Drumming
www.timespaceanddrums.com/p/constants.html

Time Space and Drums   TIME WARPS

Lesson 1

3/4, 2/4 & 6/8 Timing

Let's get straight into it and start with some 3/4 exercises. These are straightforward, so just count 3 per bar instead of the usual 4.

Exercise 1

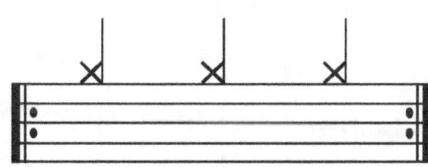

Exercise 2

Now add the bass drum on beat 1 only

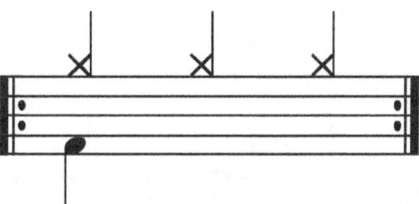

Exercise 3

Now add the SD on beat 3 only

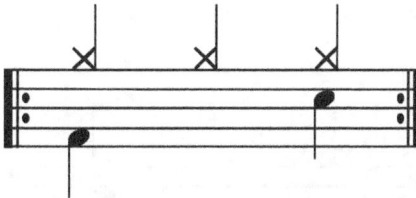

Practice this exercise until you can play it fluently, then start the next exercise by playing the RH on the ride cymbal.

Stephen Hawkins

Exercise 4

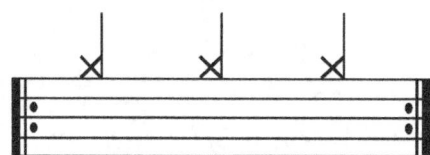

Exercise 5

This time add the LF HH on beats 1, 2 and 3.

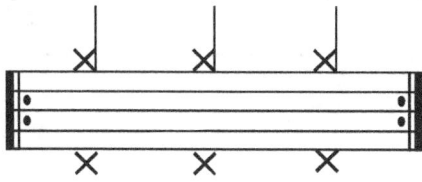

Exercise 6

Add the BD on beat 1.

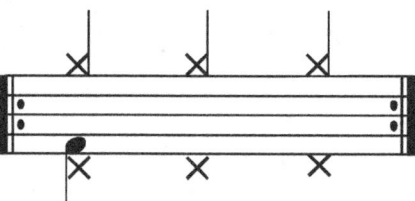

Exercise 7

And again, add the SD on beat 3.

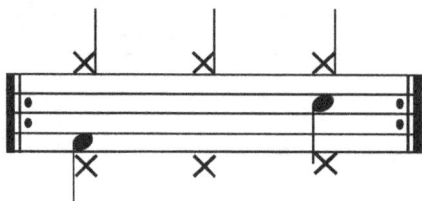

Time Space and Drums — TIME WARPS

Exercise 8

Now try these variations

Exercise 9

Exercise 10

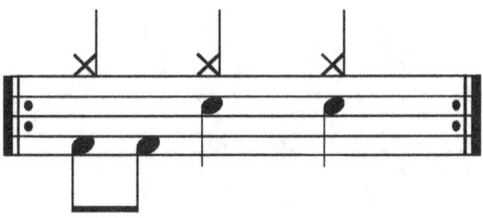

Exercise 11

Take care to play the bass drum on the last 1/16th note of the last (3rd) crotchet of the bar as accurately as possible. These beats are usually played slow, so don't rush the bass drum part.

Exercise 12

Exercise 13

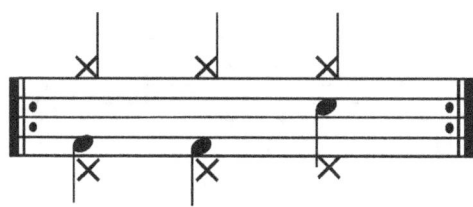

Exercise 14

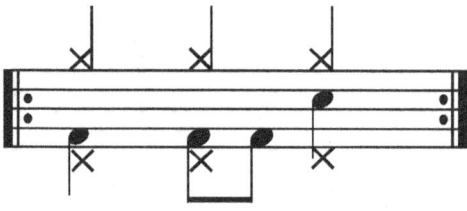

Exercise 15

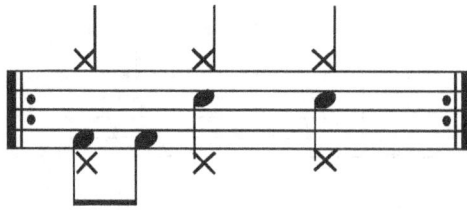

After you have worked this out in a mathematical manner again, take care to concentrate on the flow of the pulse.

Exercise 16

Exercise 17

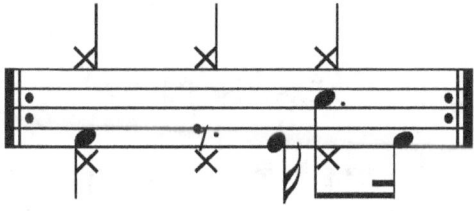

Exercise 18

This time, try using 1/8th notes on the RH HH.

Exercise 19

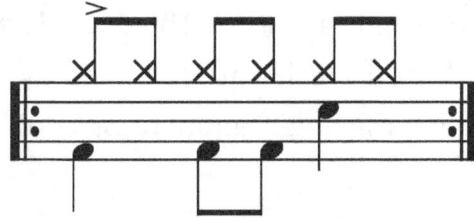

Remember at all times that the pulse is all that matters after getting the basic exercise in your muscle memory.

Exercise 20

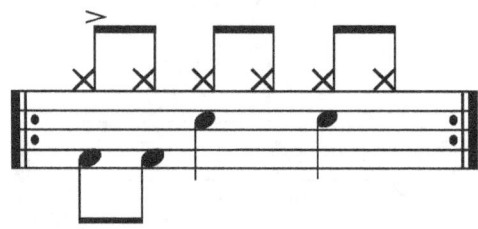

Exercise 21

Exercise 22

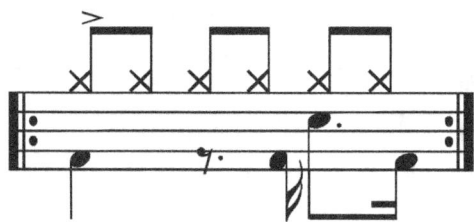

Exercise 23

This time, use a shuffle style beat on the RH HH. This sounds almost exactly like the 12/8 shuffle beat. It comprises of a dotted 1/8th note followed by a 1/16th note, which means the 1/8th note is half as long again, making it equal to 3, 1/16th notes instead of just 2.

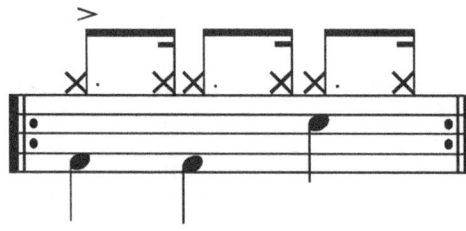

Time Warps

Exercise 24

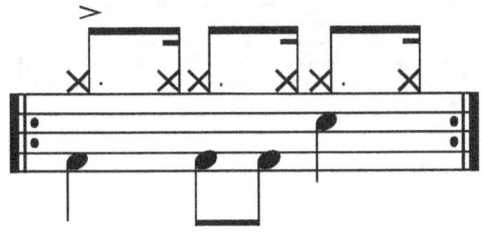

Exercise 25

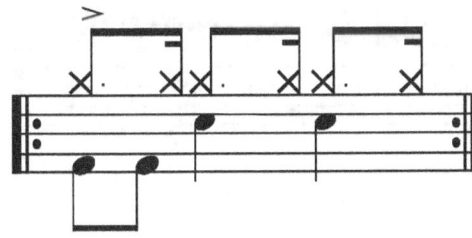

Exercise 26

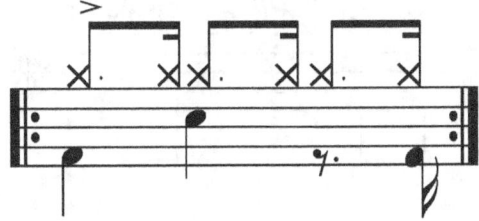

Exercise 27

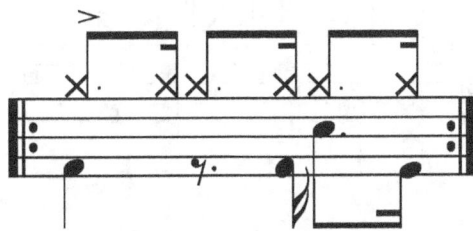

Exercise 28

This time, try some 1/16th notes on the RH HH as well as some variations.

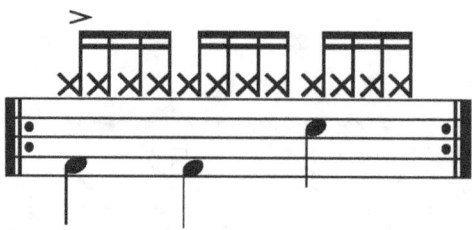

Exercise 29

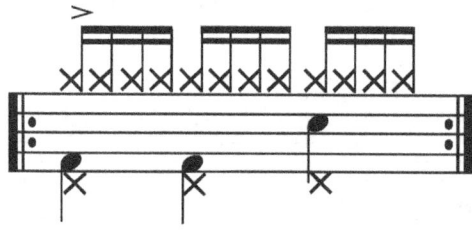

Exercise 30

Exercise 31

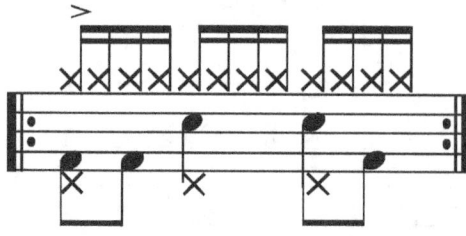

AI have added accents to the first note of each bar in some of these exercises; these are more of a guiding decision to get you to focus on making the first note of the beat whilst still keeping the flow of the pulse steady.

Exercise 32

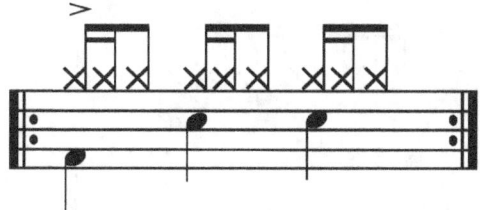

Exercise 33

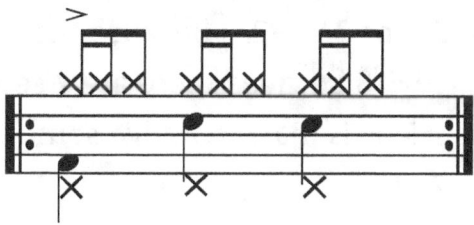

Exercise 34

Exercise 35

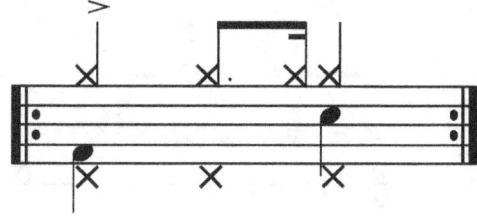

Take a look at this next exercise and see if it is easy for you to play now that you are beginning to understand drum charts and notation in regards to basic written exercises. It isn't important that you get it. I just added it as it may help you start to become a little more creative than playing exactly what is written although that is the idea, to begin with.

Exercise 36

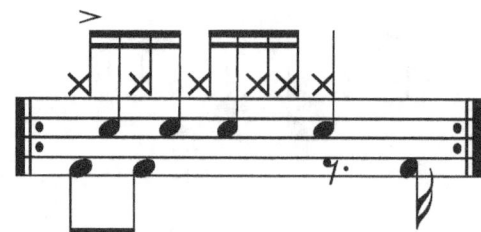

As before, perfect all of the exercises covered so far before going any further.

Our next odd time signature is 6/8 or 2/4—2/4 because there are 2 1/4 notes per bar. However, this is commonly called 6/8 because there are 2 sets of triplets comprising 3 notes within each group. The sticking is marked above some of the exercises to help you. The count should be 1 2, 2 2, 3 2 etc.

Exercise 37

Exercise 38

Now add the bass drum and HH on beats 1 and 2.

Again, don't pay too much attention to the accented first note of the bar as these are just to demonstrate the downbeat of each bar.

Exercise 39

Exercise 40

Now add the bass drum and HH on beats 1 and 2.

Exercise 41

Exercise 42

Now add the bass drum and HH on beats 1 and 2.

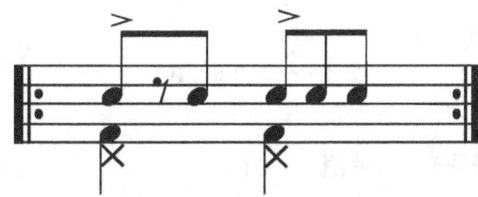

The pulse here is 1 2, 2 2, 3 2 and so on as you play through the shuffle type beats and triplets.

Exercise 43

Exercise 44

Now add the bass drum and HH on beats 1 and 2.

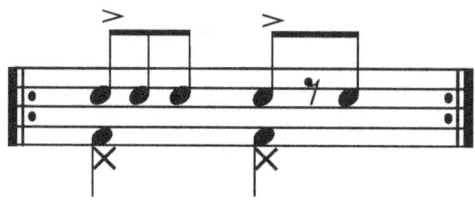

Exercise 45

This time, we'll include a flam on beats 1 and 2.

Exercise 46

Now add the bass drum and HH on beats 1 and 2.

Exercise 47

Now try these two 4 bar phrases

Exercise 48

Lesson 2

5/4 Timing

The next odd time signature is 5/4. This simply means that there are 5 ¼ notes per bar instead of the usual 4. Begin at a slow tempo before speeding up.

Exercise 1

Begin with your RH on the HH.

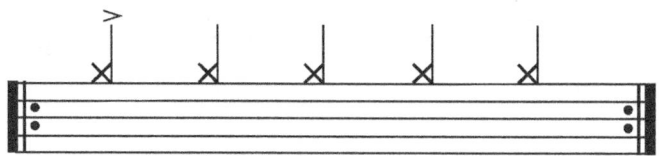

Exercise 2

Then add the BD on beats 1 and 3.

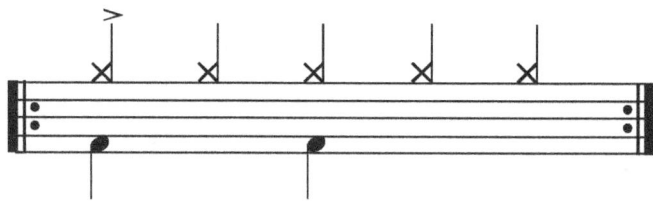

Exercise 3

Now add the SD on beats 2 and 4.

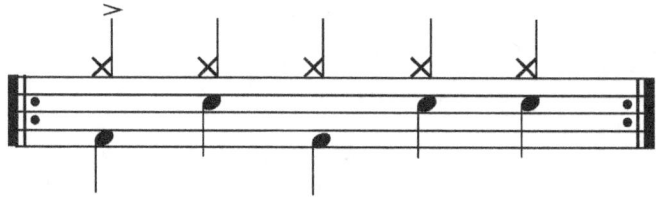

Time Space and Drums   TIME WARPS

Exercise 4

This time, play the RH on the ride cymbal.

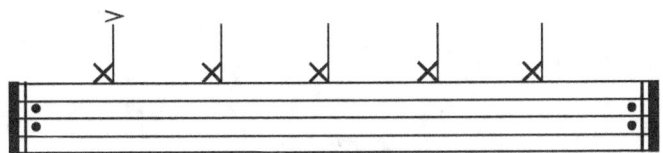

Exercise 5

Now add the LF HH on beats 1, 2, 3, 4 and 5.

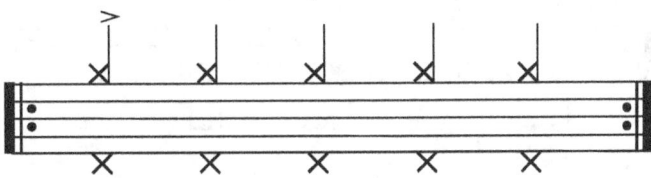

Exercise 6

Add the BD on beats 1 and 3.

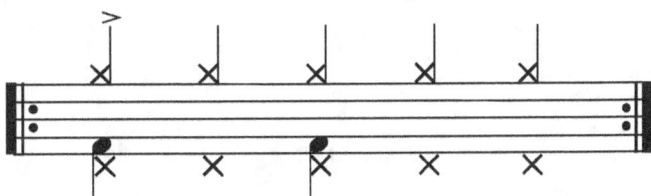

Exercise 7

Add the LH SD on beats 2, 4 and 5.

Stephen Hawkins

When you feel comfortable playing exercises 3 and 7, try the following variations.

Exercise 8

Exercise 9

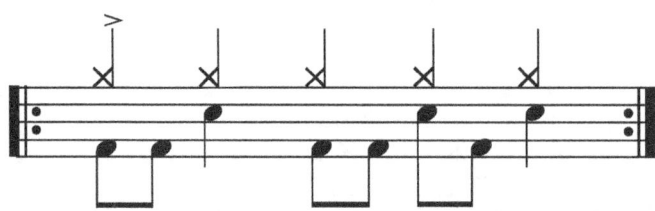

Exercise 10

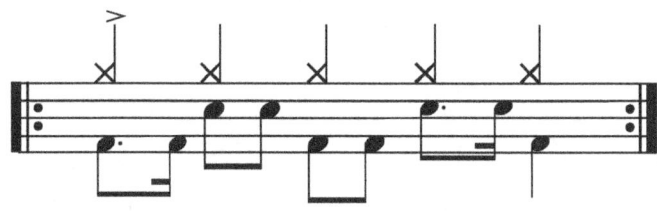

Exercise 11

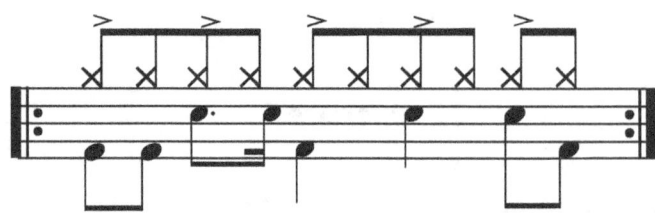

You should now be getting used to the flow of 5/4 time. You can try counting 10 instead of 5 in the previous exercise as well as the following ones but it isn't necessary.

Exercise 12

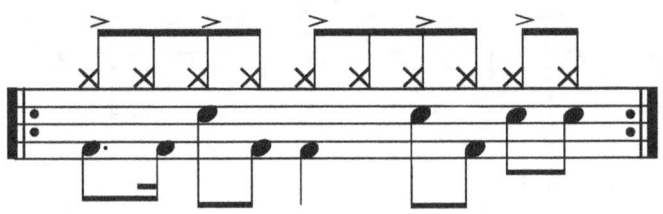

Exercise 13

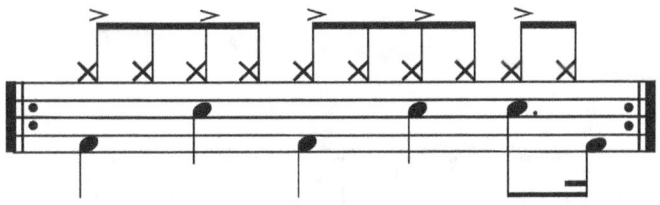

Exercise 14

Exercise 15

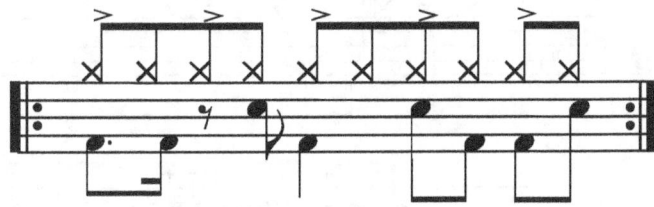

Exercise 16

This time, play a 5/4 shuffle beat

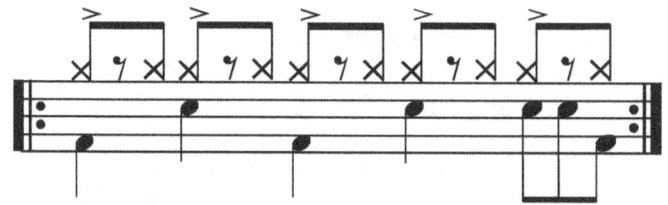

Exercise 17

Now try this 5/4 accented drum fill. Accents are covered in more detail in book 7 so realize that you don't have to play the accents. Just make sure to count and play the pulse of 5/4 time.

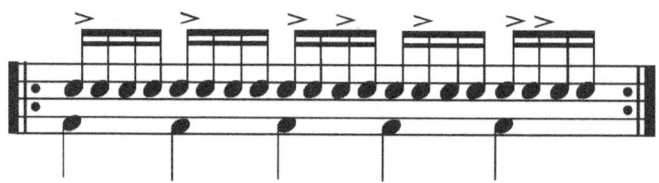

Exercise 18

Now try these 4 bar phrases in 5/4 time. Please note that I have incorporated two exercises in one here. That was intentional to make you perfect the 5/4 flow of the drum beat used in these 4 bar phrases.

Exercise 19

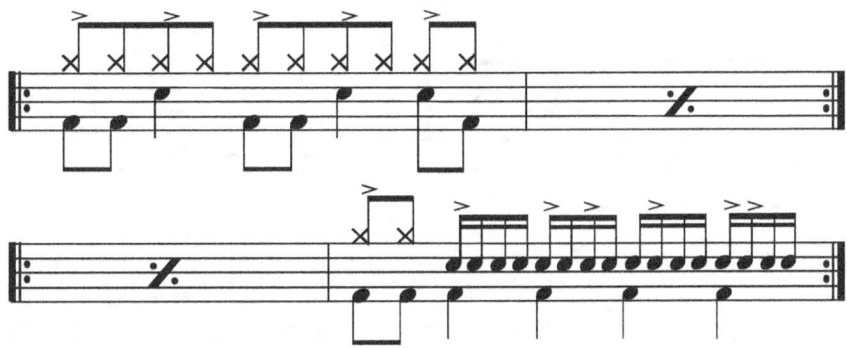

Exercise 20

Exercise 21

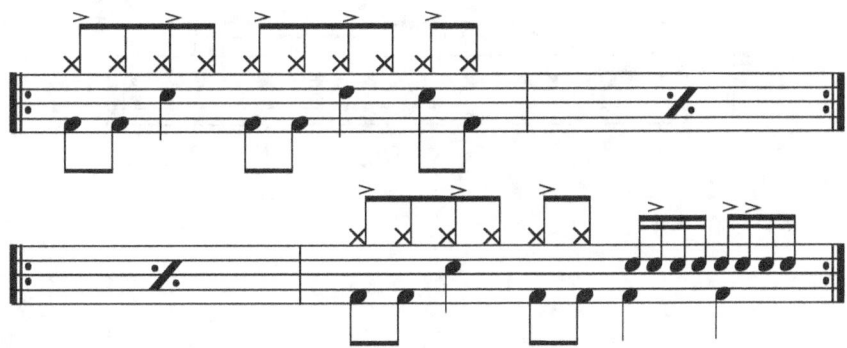

Exercise 22

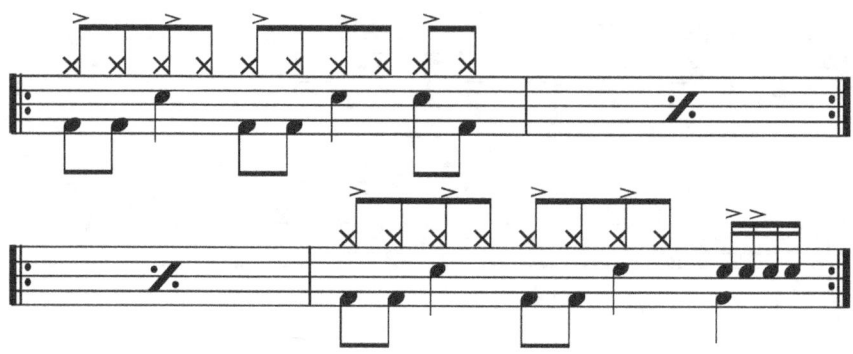

Exercise 23

Here are some more drum fill exercises

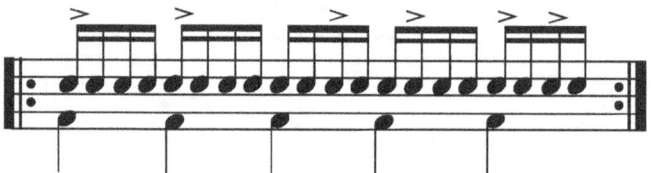

Exercise 24

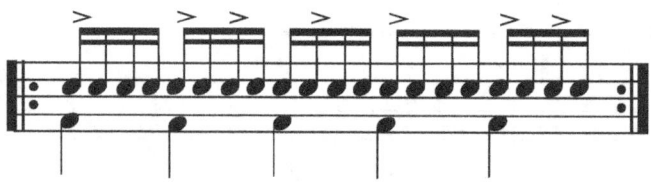

Exercise 25

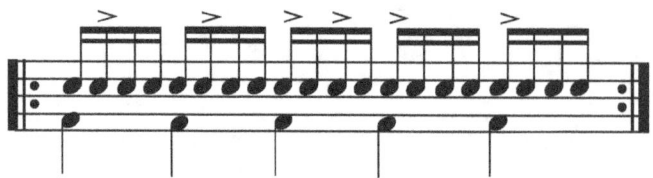

Exercise 26

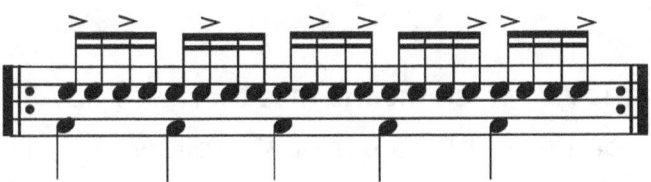

Lesson 3

7/4 Timing

This next odd time meter is 7/4 which means that there are 7 1/4 notes per bar. This should be quite easy as you simply play a bar of 4/4 followed by a bar of 3/4. You should, however, count 1, 2, 3, 4, 5, 6, 7 and treat them as 1 bar of music.

Exercise 1

Begin on the HH.

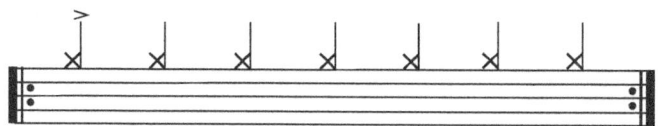

Exercise 2

Now add the BD on beats 1 and 2, 4 and 5.

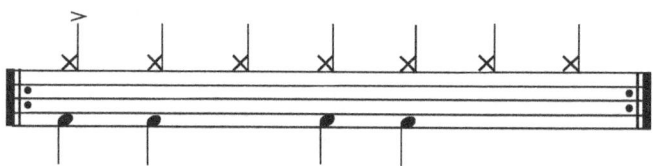

Exercise 3

Now add the SD on beats 3 and 7.

Exercise 4

Again, play the RH on the ride cymbal.

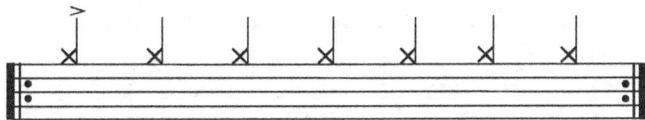

Exercise 5

Add the HH on beats 1, 2, 3, 4, 5, 6 and 7.

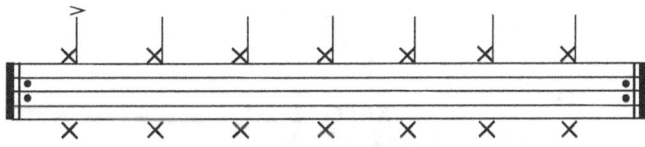

Exercise 6

Add the BD

Exercise 7

Now add the SD.

When you feel comfortable with exercises 3 and 7, you can then try the following variations.

Exercise 8

Exercise 9

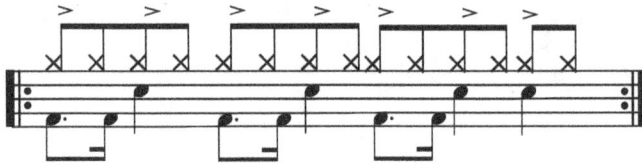

Exercise 10

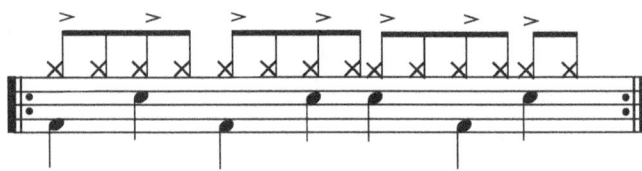

Exercise 11

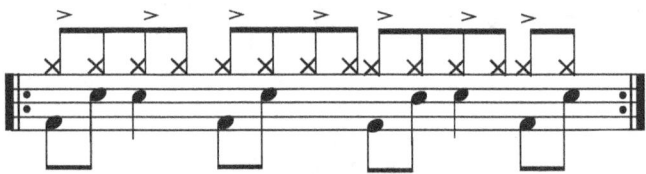

Exercise 12

Exercise 13

Exercise 14

Exercise 15

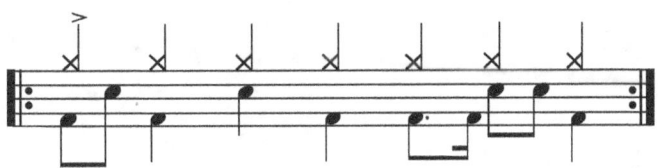

Exercise 16

Now try these accented drum fills. If you have any problems playing them, you can wait until we cover part 7 then come back to perfect these exercises in 7/4.

Exercise 17

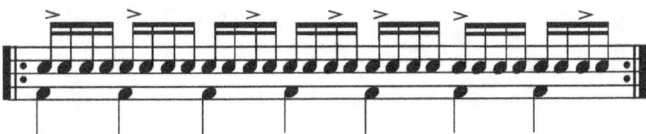

Exercise 18

Exercise 19

Lesson 4

9/4 Timing

Now let's cover some basic 9/4 rhythms. Start off by counting 1, 2, 3, 4, 5, 6, 7, 8, 9 at a slow tempo then add your RH on the HH.

Exercise 1

Exercise 2

Now add the BD on beats 1, 5 and 9.

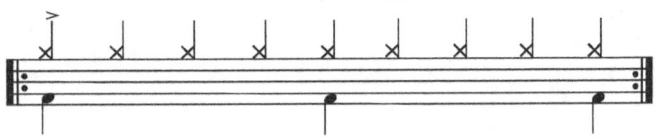

Exercise 3

Then add the LH SD on beats 3 and 7.

Exercise 4

This time, play the RH on the ride cymbal.

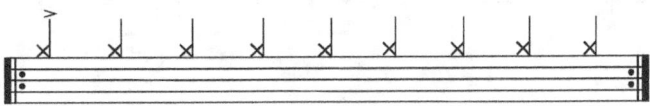

Exercise 5

Add the LF HH on 1, 2, 3, 4, 5, 6, 7, 8 and 9.

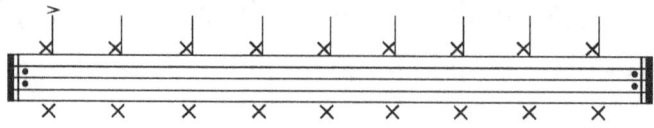

Exercise 6

Now add the BD.

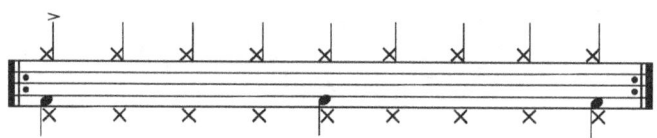

Exercise 7

Finally, add the SD.

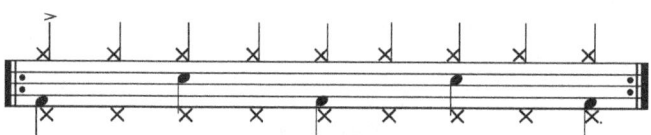

When you feel comfortable with exercises 3 and 7, try these variations:

Exercise 8

Exercise 9

Exercise 10

Lesson 5

5/8 & 7/8 Timing

This lesson covers 5/8 and 7/8. We begin with 5/8 which means there are 5 1/8th notes per bar. From this, we can deduce that 5/4 can also be called 10/8, 7/4 can be called 14/8 and so on. Although this is very rare and not technically true, it does serve as a reference.

Unless you have a programmable metronome that allows you to accent the first beat of every 5/4 bar, you will have to count 5 for yourself.

Exercise 1

Begin RH on the HH.

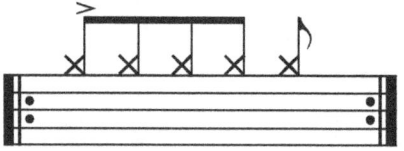

Exercise 2

Add the RF BD on beats 1 and 5.

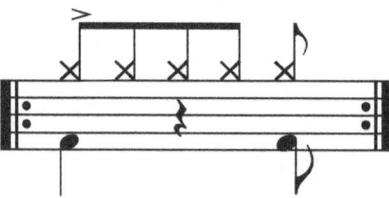

Exercise 3

Finally, add the SD on beat 3.

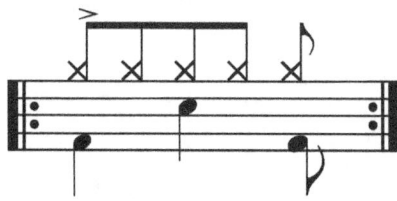

Exercise 4

Now play the RH on the ride cymbal.

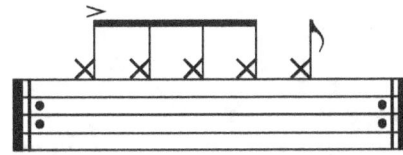

Exercise 5

Add the HH on beats 1, 3 and the 1/16th note between the 4th and 5th beats. You will have to count this LF HH rhythm very slowly to get the feel of it. When you are sure of the LF HH pattern, you should be able to feel this rhythm throughout most 5/8 drum patterns and fills. It is identical to the pattern played by the RH in the swing beat.

Listen to the CD for a demonstration.

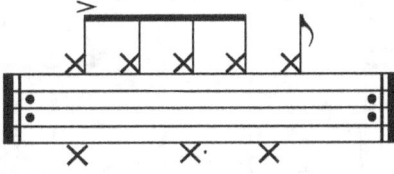

Exercise 6

Add the BD.

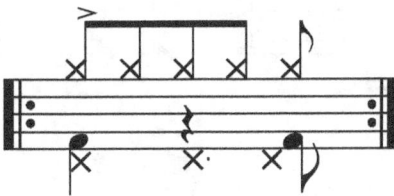

Exercise 7

Now add the SD.

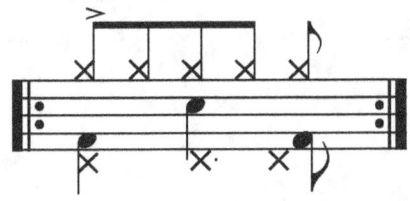

When you feel comfortable with the time feel in exercises 3 and 7, try the following variations.

Exercise 8-11

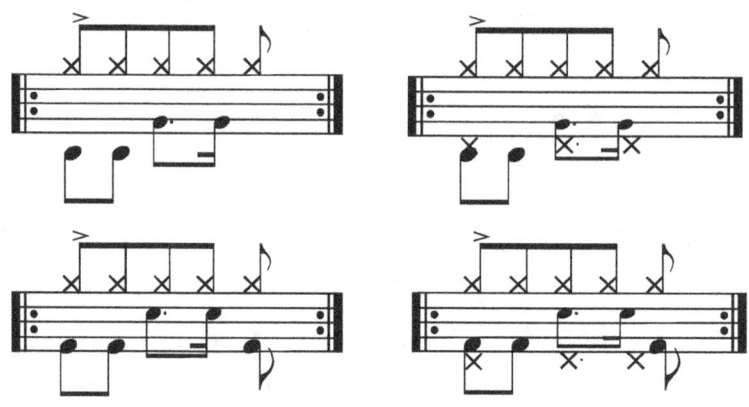

Exercise 12-15

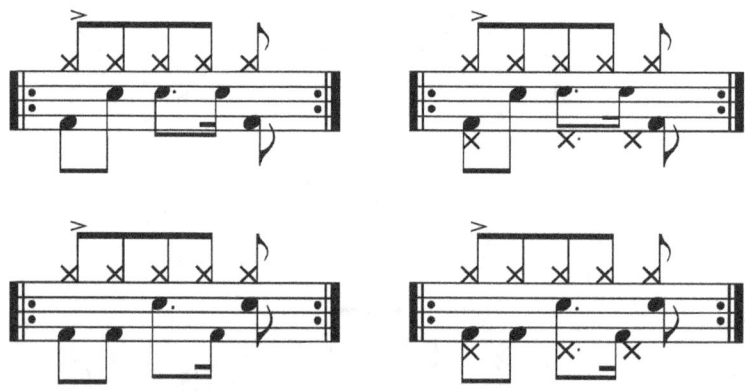

Exercise 16 & 17

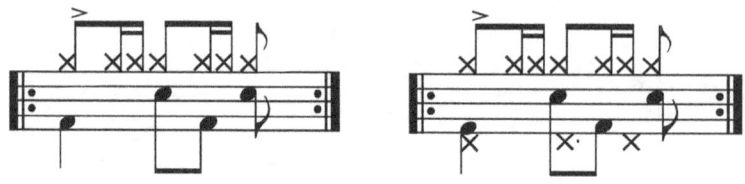

Exercise 18-21

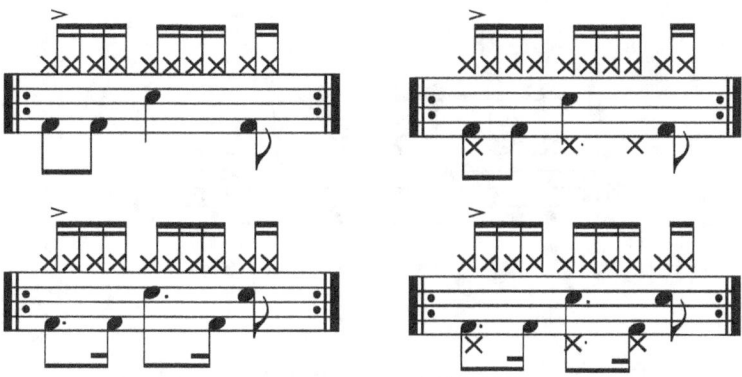

Exercise 22 & 23

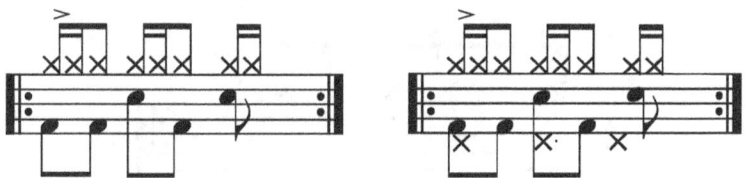

Now let's try some 7/8 patterns this should be straightforward after mastering 5/8.

Exercise 24

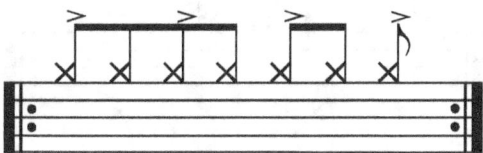

Exercise 25

Add the BD on beats 1 and 5.

Exercise 26

Now add the SD on beats 3 and 7.

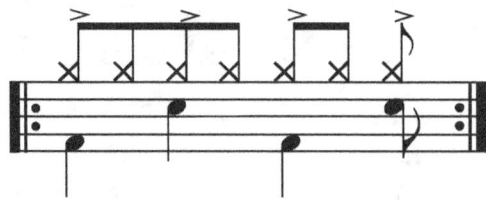

Exercise 27

This time, play the RH on the ride cymbal.

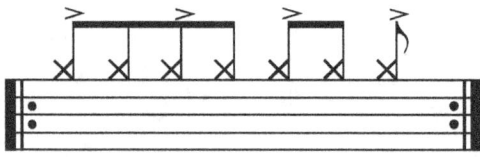

Exercise 28

Add the LF HH.

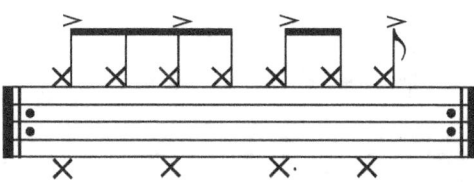

Exercise 29

Add the BD.

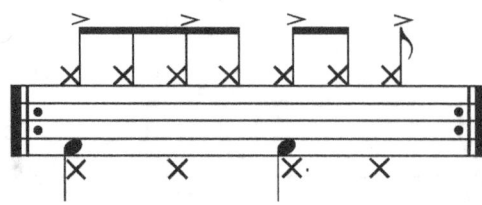

Exercise 30

Add the SD.

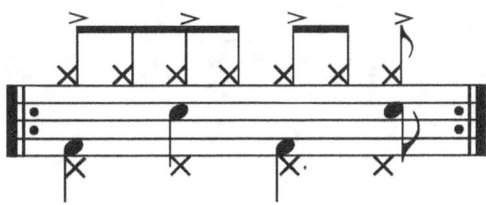

Now try these variations:

Exercise 31

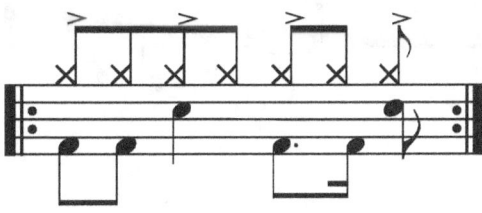

Exercise 32

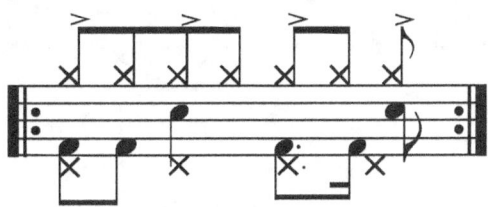

Exercise 33

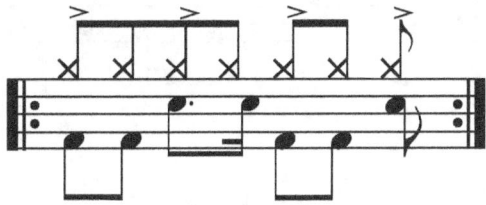

Make sure that you are comfortable with the previous exercises before trying the next slightly more difficult exercise. Saying that, once you have gotten this far, you should be okay, so just keep taking your time. There is no rush.

Exercise 34

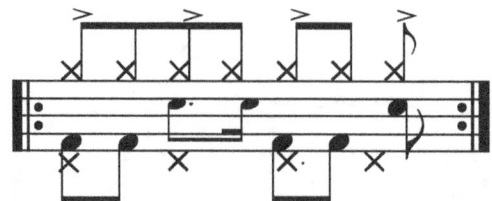

Exercise 35

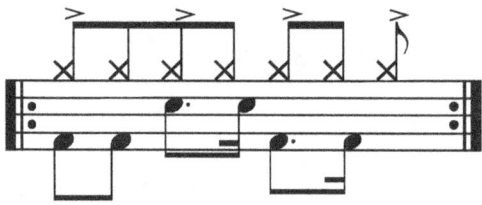

Exercise 36

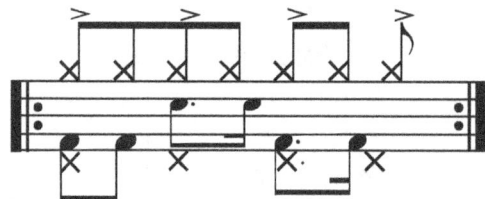

Exercise 37

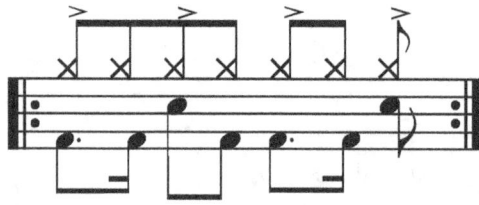

Exercise 38

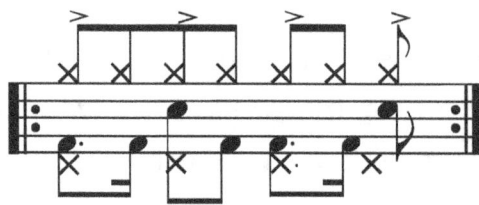

Exercise 39

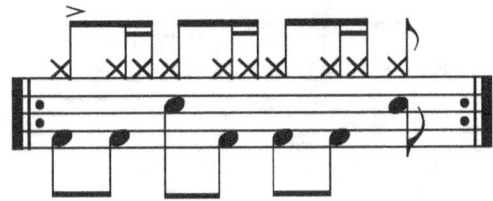

Exercise 40

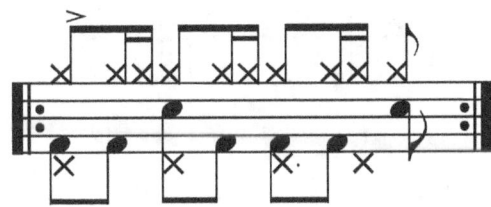

Exercise 41

Exercise 42

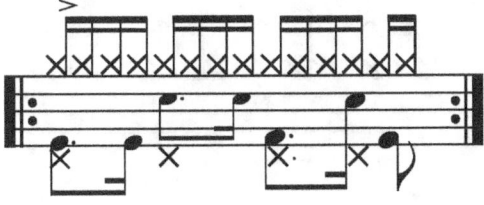

Exercise 42-B Not recorded

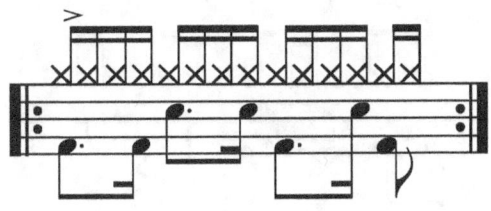

Exercise 42-C Not recorded

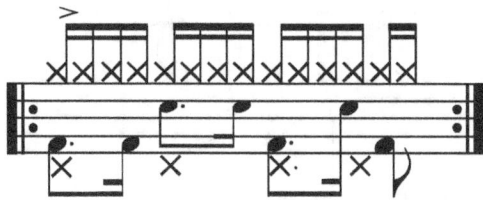

Exercise 43

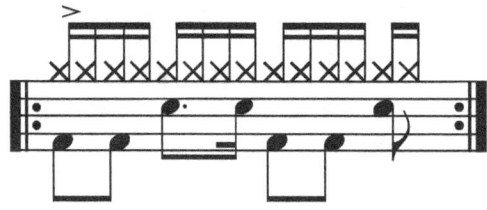

Exercise 44

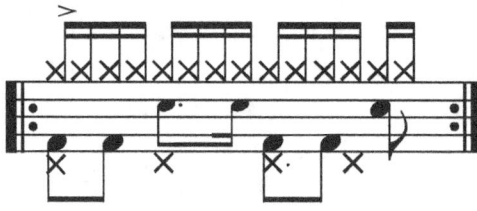

Exercise 45

Exercise 46

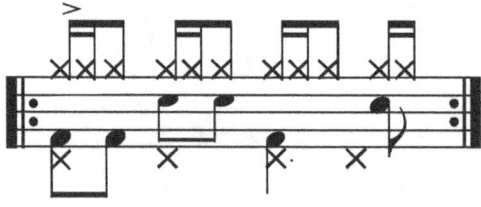

Lesson 6

9/8 Timing

This final lesson deals with 9/8. Again, this should be pretty straightforward after mastering 5/8 and 7/8. So, let's get down to it.

Exercise 1

Begin as usual on the HH.

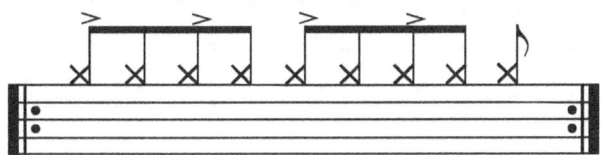

Exercise 2

Add the BD on beats 1, 3, 5 and 8.

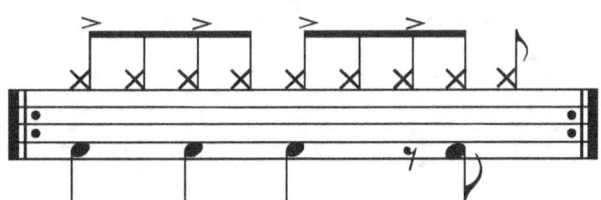

Exercise 3

Add the SD on beats 4, 7 and 9.

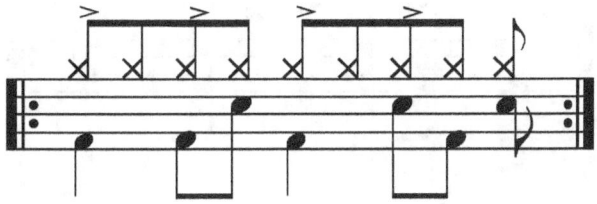

Time Space and Drums — TIME WARPS

Exercise 4

Play the RH RC.

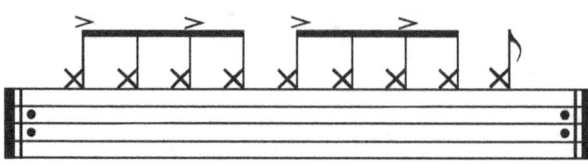

Exercise 5

Add the LF HH.

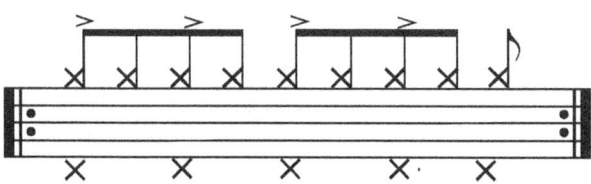

Exercise 6

Add the BD.

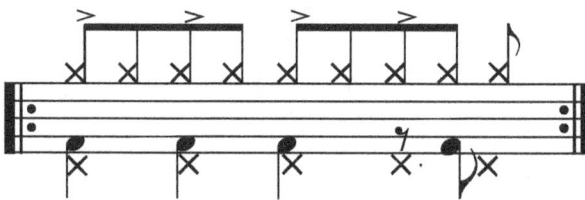

Exercise 7

Now add the SD.

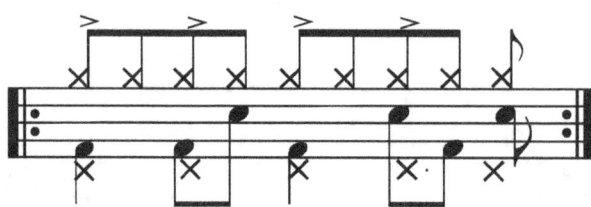

Now try these variations:

Exercise 8

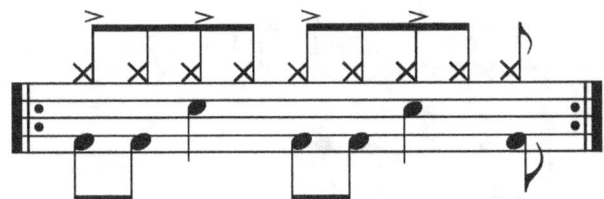

Exercise 9

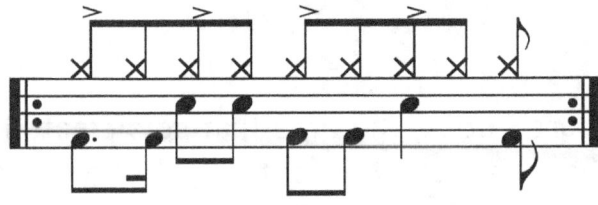

Exercise 10

Exercise 11

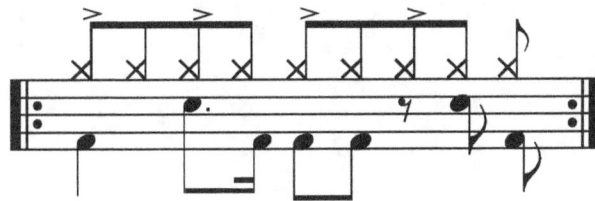

Exercise 12

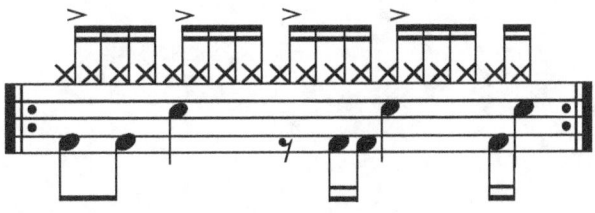

Exercise 13

TIME WARPS

As suggested within this part 5 book, the time that gets created by a drummer can vary quite a bit. A time warp then is a metaphor for those changes and varying time signatures that stray away from the normal flow of 4/4 music. A time warp is an imaginary spatial distortion that allows time travel in fiction, or a hypothetical form of time dilation or contraction. These time warps all stem from the theory of Einstein's general relativity.

Although time travel is a common theme throughout science fiction novels in our metaphor, we are speaking less of time travel and more in regards of distortions in space. Stephen Hawking called this spacetime, where time could be bent either from one place in the universe to another or from one point in time to another.

This then fits our analogy of warping the standardised 4/4 common time into all kinds of distortions or warps such as 5/4, 7/4 and so on.

RUDIMENTARY

Flam Exercises

So, let us just presume that you have now been practicing the flams we covered in book 4 for a few weeks now; therefore, you should be getting used to playing them using just right-hand flams, left-hand flams and alternate flams.

We are not going to add another rudiment at this stage and are instead going to set a few exercises for you to practice flams further.

Although these exercises will move into the intermediate level, they are still fairly simple, depending on your skill level and perspective.

The exercises we are going to cover are $1/8^{th}$ note exercises and triplet exercises and we are going to make this basic, simply because they form the foundation on much more complex exercises which I will suggest later. But for now, let's begin with the first exercise.

$1/8^{th}$ Note Rhythm and Quarter Note Flams

As the heading suggests, this first exercise covers the basic 8 x $1/8^{th}$ notes in a bar but with the 1/4 notes playing flams.

First, play the $1/8^{th}$ note rhythm using alternate sticking like this:

R L, R L, R L, R L.

Then add the flams to the 1/4 notes using just right-hand flams like this:

ʟR L, ʟR L, ʟR L, ʟR L.

Next, try playing the same exercise using alternate flams with a right-hand flam on beat 1, a left-hand flam on beat 2 and a left-hand flam on beat 4 like this:

ʟR L, ʀL R, ʟR L, ʀL R.

1/8th Note Triplets and Quarter Note Flams

Again, as the heading suggests, this first exercise covers the basic 12 x 1/8th note triplets in a bar as covered in book 2, but with the 1/4 notes playing flams.

Begin by playing the 1/8th note triplet pattern using alternate sticking like this:

R L R,   L R L,   R L R,   L R L.

This time, playing triplets with the flams on the 1/4 notes forces the sticking to become: R L R,   R L R,   R L R,   R L R. So after you get used to practicing and playing that sticking, try adding the right-hand flams like this:

ʟR L R,   ʟR L R,   ʟR L R,   ʟR L R.

And then, of course, you can try practicing the same with the left-hand leading, playing just left-hand flams like this:

ʀL R L,   ʀL R L,   ʀL R L,   ʀL R L.

Then again, when you have practiced this and become more comfortable with the sticking and sound, you can try alternate flams with triplets like this:

ʟR L R,   ʀL R L,   ʟR L R,   ʀL R L.

Of course, all of the exercises would look like the following written exercise if I had written them in a musical notation form. However, I thought the understanding of the exercise was more important at the beginning stage than seeing the written exercise as shown below. And, as before, you can see the small grace note before each 1/4 note.

ʟR L R, ʀL R L, ʟR L R, ʀL R L.

Different Practice Approach

If you find the previous exercises easy then you might want to rewrite them in an exercise book. Play the flams on the second beat of the triplet and then again on the third beat of the triplet. You can then rewrite them and create combinations playing the first note of the first set of triplets then the second note of the triplets then the third and so on.

You could also try writing the exercise playing the flam on the first note of every first $1/16^{th}$ note in a set of 4 x $1/16^{th}$ notes and so on.

Having said that, try not to get too off-track if you have been playing drums less than a year as it is more important at this stage to get a better and more solid understanding and control over the basics.

We previously focused on a single rudiment in each of the Time Space and Drums series books covered so far:

- Part 1 of this series covered the single stroke roll,
- Part 2 covered the triplet rudiment,
- Part 3 covered the double stroke roll,
- Part 4 covered the flam.

And this fifth book in the series is centered around further integrating the rudiments covered so far, and getting them just a little bit better. It is important to revisit each rudiment section within each of the books in the series and establish a practice schedule for the rudiment sections. For every hour you practice rhythms and beats you should practice at least 30 minutes just playing rudiments. But by playing, I really mean practicing and improving which means highly focused and to some extent, critical thinking practice. Or as I like to call it... Scientific!

To begin with, you can spend the 30 minutes on a single rudiment and alternate them over the week until you begin to build strength and speed. Here again, I refer to speed simply as the fluidity of your playing or the smoothness and not necessarily playing at a million miles per hour. That will come to the degree that you perfect the rudiments at slower tempos concentrating entirely on the flow of the rudiments.

Featured Drummer

Terry Bozzio

If you want to hear a drummer who has completely stepped away from what everybody else does when they sit at a drum kit, then meet Terry Bozzio. Terry literally brings the whole orchestra to a drum kit.

To give you an idea, I believe one of his kits includes 5 hi-hat pedals alone and contains a total of 22 pedals. There are 8 Bass Drums, 26 Toms, 2 Snare Drums and a massive 53 cymbals.

As I write, I have struck a blank because it is so hard to get my head around the fact that someone could do what he does on the drum kit. He actually plays classical pieces as the kit is tuned to a musical scale.

Okay, so why Terry Bozzio? Well, apart from what I have just said about his kit and unique playing style that goes with it alone, which I believe begins to move away from drumming just a little and into the realms of being a percussive piano type instrument, he is guilty of playing some completely awesome odd time drumming.

In particular, and my absolute favorite album of all time, in his early days in 1979 he played for a band called UK. Every single one of the UK albums was awesome but in particular, I am pointing to the album Danger Money.

The time signature changes in the UK albums are completely awesome to put it bluntly. The UK album was the first album I listened to and was addicted to counting along to. That is very strange for me to do as I have never really got along with counting notes and beats. I was all about creating singing bass line type patterns that ran parallel to the count... in my head. Humming if you will.

Terry also featured in over twenty-six Frank Zappa albums. Frank Zappa was my favorite artist of all time simply because his music was so diverse and contained more time changes than any book on time changes. I myself much prefer the challenge of Franks, as well as bands such as UK than the mainstream pop music because of the challenge they presented. I also don't think my ears are conducive to Normalized Timbre-less music.

Bill Bruford

I couldn't move past this odd time foundation course without also mentioning Bill Bruford, another of my favorite drummers for basically the same reasons as Terry Bozzio. They both played for UK at some point and had a very similar style although Terry did move away from that style center when he added 53 cymbals to his drum kit setup.

The Bill Bruford band called Bruford created three of my top 10 albums: Feel Good to Me, Gradually Going Tornado and One of a Kind.

Those albums have a special affinity to odd time playing and fantastic drumming. I could quite easily stop typing and place all those albums on a loop and listen to them for the next week solid. And I would never get bored because the complexity of the music and drumming is so diverse that it does not have the same effect as repetitive 4-chord songs that repeat several times within themselves.

One time listening to those types of repetitive music and I need a break from music altogether. But that is just me. Don't get me wrong, I have listened to many pop style bands over the years but now it all seems too bland for my ears.

I hope that you decide to invest in yourself and listen to some of the albums I mention here as I am sure you will love the drumming, at the very least. You could maybe get a few inspirations of your own in regard to your own style of drumming and the direction you wish to move in.

Conclusion

As a final note, I would just like to add that what goes for 4/4 also goes for other time signatures and that is, the 1/4 notes should be accented up to the point where the 1/16th note LF HH is played. This sounds confusing but you will soon get the idea through analyzing the above exercises and a little experimentation. The point is that the LF is conveying a pulse. That pulse should also be accented on the RH pattern, be it played on the HH or on the ride cymbal using the bell of the cymbal to play the accents.

That said, I will leave you to get on with the work. See you next time. Until then, master the art of playing in odd time signatures.

S. J. Hawkins.

Closing Note:

The Time Space and Drums series is intended as a complete program from Part 1 to Part 12. It is strongly advised that you follow the program in order of the parts as they integrate and build on each other. The only thing I can now add is to practice each exercise until you have them all mastered. Mastery comes from paying attention to the most basic fundamentals already covered in each of the exercises within this book.

Once you have perfected each exercise you may like to try them left-handed but that may take time depending on your current skill level.

Free Audio Demonstrations

Please don't forget to visit the following URL to download audio demonstrations of every exercise in this book as soon as possible. You will then receive soma additional tips and guidance through the included essence emails.

https://timespaceanddrums.com/tsd-5ot.html

Second Classified Document

Universal Constants - Philosophy of Drumming
www.timespaceanddrums.com/p/constants.html

What's Next

Thank you for choosing Time Space and Drums as one of your learning tools. I hope you enjoyed the process. You can explore more of the series in Space to Play, the sixth book in the series by searching for **"Write Your Own Drum Charts"** at your favorite bookstore.

Share Your Experience

If you have a moment, please review this Odd Time Drumming Development book at the store where you bought it. Help other drummers and tell them why you enjoyed the book or what could be improved. Thank you!

Thank you again dear reader and I hope we meet again between the pages of another book. Remember, You rock!

Other Books by The Author

Modern Drumming Concepts
Rock Drumming Foundation Series part. (Six in-depth Drum Lessons).
Jazz Drumming Foundation Series part. (Six in-depth Drum Lessons).
Rock Drumming Development Series part. (Six in-depth Drum Lessons).
Jazz Drumming Development Series part. (Six in-depth Drum Lessons).
Odd Time Drumming Foundation Series part. (Six in-depth Drum Lessons).
Accents and Phrasing Series part. (Four in-depth Drum Lessons).
Basic Latin Drumming Foundation Series part. (Four in-depth Drum Lessons).

 Have you ever thought about what it would feel like to make a living as a pro drummer?

If so, then visit the Drum Coach website. I might be for YOU!

The purpose of the Drum Coach blog is not only to provide drummers with valuable information but also to help them share their passions.

The Drum Coach provides all types of drumming information from beginner lessons right up to professional level playing skills, as well as personal self*(drummer)*-improvement essentials – there's something here no matter your skill level!

Some of the most important information on this website comes from my personal experiences as a percussionist and musician for over 35 years. So, I invite you to take advantage of the Drum Coach Experience, whose aim is to provide high-quality, on-demand information for drummers as they travel along their journey to achieve their personal drumming goals and ambitions.

Our commitment to our readers is always 100%! If you have any problems, questions, or concerns, just let us know and we'll help you take care of the situation as quickly as possible.

And remember to **Stay In Time!** and continue to **Rock!**

www.ingramcontent.com/pod-product-compliance
Lightning Source LLC
Chambersburg PA
CBHW081628100526

44590CB00021B/3645